The Middle East

ISRAEL AND PALESTINE

John King

www.raintreepublishers.co.uk
Visit our website to find out more information about **Raintree** books.

To order:
☎ Phone 44 (0) 1865 888112
 Send a fax to 44 (0) 1865 314091
 Visit the Raintree bookshop at **www.raintreepublishers.co.uk** to browse
our catalogue and order online.

 Produced for Raintree by
Monkey Puzzle Media Ltd.
Gissing's Farm, Fressingfield
Suffolk IP21 5SH, UK

First published in Great Britain by Raintree,
Halley Court, Jordan Hill, Oxford OX2 8EJ,
part of Harcourt Education.
Raintree is a registered trademark of Harcourt
Education Ltd.

Edited by Jenny Siklós and Paul Mason
Designed by Tim Mayer
Picture Research by Lynda Lines and Frances Bailey
Production by Duncan Gilbert
The consultant, Dr. Robert Stern, works as a part-time
analyst for the US State Department, primarily as part
of the War on Terror. He is a former Associate
Director for Counter-Terrorism.

Originated by Modern Age
Printed and bound in China by South China
Printing Company Ltd

ISBN 1 844 43204 1
10 09 08 07 06
10 9 8 7 6 5 4 3 2 1

British Library Cataloguing in Publication Data
King, John, 1939-
    Israel and Palestine. - (The Middle East)
    1.Arab-Israeli conflict - Juvenile literature
    2.Arab-Israeli conflict - 1993- - Peace - Juvenile
    literature
    I.Title
    956.9'405

Acknowledgements
The author and publisher are grateful to the
following for permission to reproduce copyright
material: AKG-Images p. **6** (Erich Lessing); Camera
Press pp. **10**, **18** (Gianni Muratore), **28** (Kevin
Unger); Corbis pp. **1** (Ricki Rosen), **5** (Ricki
Rosen/SABA), **9**, **12** (David S. Bover), **15** (David
Rubinger), **19** (Genevieve Chauvel/Sygma), **31**
(Ricki Rosen/SABA), **33** (Antoine Gyori/Sygma),
37 (Peter Turnley), **38** (Patrick Robert/Sygma),
39 (David Rubinger), **40** Ron Sachs/Sygma), **46**
(Havakuk Levison); Empics p. **4** (EPA); Getty
Images pp. **16** (David Rubinger), **22** (Daniel
Rosenbaum), **23** (Keystone), **25** (David
Rubinger), **26** (Uzi Keren/GPO), **29** (David
Rubinger), **30** (David Rubinger), **35** (Nabil Ismail),
36 (MPI), **43** (Stephen Jaffe), **44** (David
Silverman); Popperfoto.com p. **20**; Reuters pp.
42 (Khaled Zighari), **45** (Reinhard Krause), **47**
(Gadi Kabalo); Rex Features **32** (SIPA), **34** (SIPA);
Topfoto.co.uk pp. **13**, **14**, **21**, **24**, **27**; Werner
Forman Archive **7**.

Cover photograph shows a Palestinian youth
throwing stones at an Israeli tank in Hebron, 2003
(Empics/EPA).

Map illustrations by Encompass Graphics Ltd.

Every effort has been made to contact copyright
holders of any material reproduced in this book.
Any omissions will be rectified in subsequent
printings if notice is given to the publishers.

The paper used to print this book comes from
sustainable resources.

Contents

Some words are shown in **bold**, like this. You can find out what they mean by looking in the Glossary.

Death at the Crossroads

On 30 September 2000, a 12-year-old Palestinian boy named Mohammed al-Durrah and his father Jamal were in a taxi returning home from a visit to a used car lot in Gaza. The driver refused to cross the road junction at Netzarim. A confrontation between stone-throwing Palestinian youths and Israeli soldiers had started. The troops had started firing at the youths, and the taxi driver did not want to risk being shot.

The confrontation was being filmed by a Palestinian TV cameraman. Jamal and his son tried to walk across the street, but had to shelter against a wall. Even so, Mohammed was hit by several shots and collapsed. He died on his way to Gaza's Al-Shifa Hospital. His father Jamal was also hit, but later recovered. Israel later made an official apology for Mohammed's death.

Mohammed al-Durrah and his father cower against a wall in Gaza, as they come under fire from Israeli soldiers defending the Netzarim road junction.

Violence had exploded in the previous two days. On 28 September an Israeli politician, Ariel Sharon, made a high profile visit to the **Temple Mount** in East Jerusalem.

Ariel Sharon (centre) at the Temple Mount on 28 September 2000. His visit sparked off the troubles known as the Al-Aqsa Intifada.

Temple Mount is an important religious site for both Jews and Muslims. Sharon wanted to show that, as an Israeli and Jewish leader, he could go wherever he wanted in the Holy Land, even to areas claimed by the Palestinians as their own. This sparked off the **Al-Aqsa Intifada**, the latest phase of the decades-long conflict between Israel and the Palestinians.

VIOLENCE AGAINST ISRAELIS

Many Israeli children also died in the violence following the outbreak of the Al-Aqsa Intifada. For example, in August 2003, at least five children were among eighteen people killed in a 'suicide bombing'. A Palestinian militant had blown himself up on a bus. Medics had to carry away children with blood-smeared faces, and one baby girl died in a hospital before doctors could find her parents.

Two Peoples, One Land

How did the bitter conflict between Jewish Israelis and Palestinians begin? The conflict first developed at the end of the 19th and the beginning of the 20th centuries. At this time Jews began to settle in lands that were occupied by Palestinian Arabs. The two groups have struggled ever since for land and the right to live on it.

The Jewish claim to the land of Israel goes back to biblical days. Until the end of the first century CE, the Jews lived in the area now known as Israel, which was then a province of the Roman Empire. The Jews rebelled against Roman rule, but they were crushed by the Romans. Some fled to other countries, while others stayed behind. Since that time, most of the world's Jews have lived in different countries around the world.

In this 17th-century painting by Nicolas Poussin, the Roman Emperor Titus is destroying the Jewish Temple in Jerusalem in 70 CE.

The Arabs also have lived in the same region for centuries. After the Prophet Mohammed founded the Islamic faith in 610 CE, Muslim armies conquered much of the old Roman Empire in the East. These new Muslim territories included the land known as Palestine, now Israel. Most Palestinians became Muslims. Virtually everyone came to speak the Arabic language, as Palestinians still do today.

This painting shows Arab life as seen by a Muslim artist from the 16th century. A great feast is being prepared.

The British Mandate

After 1921 Palestine was governed by Great Britain, under a **mandate** from the **League of Nations**. During the British Mandate, thousands of Jews from Europe settled in Palestine. This soon led to confrontations between Arabs and Jews.

Britain divided its mandated territory into two parts (see map below). To the east of the River Jordan the British created the state of Transjordan. West of the river, they kept direct control over the territory of Palestine.

Before **World War I** some Jews had started to leave Europe for Palestine, where Jews were already living in Jerusalem and other cities. Many of the new arrivals had been inspired by the **Zionist movement**. Zionists campaigned for the creation of a Jewish community in Palestine, or 'Zion'. The Zionist leader, Theodor Herzl, said that the Jews should return to Palestine, their ancient home, where they could live in a land of their own.

THE MANDATES

The League of Nations Mandates were the controls Britain and France maintained over the Middle East after World War I. When World War I broke out in 1914, the **Ottoman Empire**, the Turkish power that ruled the region, fought on the side of Germany. When the war ended in 1918, the defeated Turks lost control of their Arab territories. In 1921 the League of Nations, a similar organization to today's United Nations, asked Britain and France to rule the Arab lands of the Middle East as mandated territories, until the Arabs were 'ready for independence'.

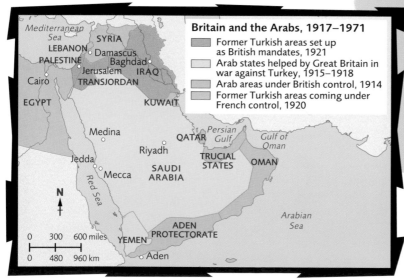

Britain and the Arabs, 1917–1971

- Former Turkish areas set up as British mandates, 1921
- Arab states helped by Great Britain in war against Turkey, 1915–1918
- Arab areas under British control, 1914
- Former Turkish areas coming under French control, 1920

This map shows the extent of British influence in the Arab world following World War I.

During World War I, the British Foreign Secretary, Arthur Balfour, said that Britain would accept Jewish immigration into Palestine. As a result, in the 1920s and 1930s more Jews came to Palestine. In 1914 there had been 80,000 Jews in Palestine and 500,000 Palestinian Arabs. By 1948 the Jewish population had reached 650,000 out of a total of 2,000,000. A third of Palestine's people was now Jewish.

The growing Jewish population made the Palestinians increasingly worried about losing control of their lands. In 1936 there was a major Palestinian revolt against the Jews and the British authorities. The revolt was crushed.

In 1939 **World War II** began. The USA, the UK and their allies were victorious in 1945. The Jews in Europe had suffered terribly during the war: millions of Jews had been murdered by the Nazis. As a result, the idea of a Jewish homeland in Palestine had become even more popular.

> ❝ His Majesty's government view with favour the establishment in Palestine of a national home for the Jewish people [though] nothing shall be done which may prejudice [harm] the ... non-Jewish communities. ❞
> *(The **Balfour Declaration**, 2 November 1917)*

British troops attempt to drive back Palestinian rioters in the Old City of Jerusalem in 1936. The riots were protests against the British for allowing Jewish immigration into Palestine.

Israel is Born

The murder of six million Jews by German forces during World War II became known as the **Holocaust**. This appalling act increased the Jewish desire for a country of their own. But there was still conflict in Palestine between Arabs and Jews.

In 1947 the UK said it intended to return the Mandate to the United Nations, which had been set up after the war to replace the League of Nations. In November 1947 the United Nations decided to divide Palestine into two parts, one each for the Arab and Jewish communities. Jerusalem was to be a separate International Zone under United Nations supervision.

On 14 May 1948, after the end of the British Mandate, the Jewish leader David Ben Gurion proclaimed the

THE HOLOCAUST
During the course of World War II, the Nazi regime in Germany attempted to exterminate the Jewish population of Europe. Jews from all over Europe were sent to death camps in Germany and Poland, where most were killed. Some Jews were killed in other places too. As a result of the Holocaust, six million Jews lost their lives.

Israelis celebrate the declaration of the State of Israel on 14 May 1948.

existence of the State of Israel. Ben Gurion then became Israel's first prime minister. Support for Israel came from US President, Harry Truman, and from the American Jewish community.

The Arabs refused to accept the division of Palestine. There were more Arabs than Jews in the 'Jewish' part, and Arabs owned most of the land. The Arabs launched an attack on the Jews. Neighbouring Arab countries also sent in troops. The Jewish defence forces were well prepared, and fought back hard. Jewish weapons were paid for by international supporters. Jewish forces captured most of Palestine, including half of Jerusalem. The Arabs kept the Old City.

By January 1949, the fighting was over, though neither side declared peace. More than 300,000 Palestinian Arabs had fled their homes in June 1948, and hundreds of thousands more left later. These were the first Palestinian refugees.

> ❝ Victory in the War of Independence, glorious as it was, cost us 5,000 and more of our precious lives. But if ever Jewish lives were not lost in vain, it was then. ❞
>
> (Israel, Years of Challenge, *by David Ben Gurion*)

Below left: The areas allotted to Arabs and Jews under the partition plan approved by the United Nations.

Below right: Areas held by Jews and Arabs during the conflict of 1948–1949.

The United Nations Partition Plan, 1947

- Proposed Jewish State
- Proposed Arab State
- Jerusalem UN zone
- ····· Modern borders

The Israeli War of Independence, 1948–1949

- Israeli control, June 1948
- Israeli conquest, June–Nov 1948
- Israeli conquest, Nov 1948–Jan 1949
- Israeli occupation and withdrawal, 1949
- Israel border, 1949–1967

Palestinian Refugees

According to the United Nations, over 725,000 refugees fled or were forced from their homes in Palestine during the fighting between April and December 1948. Of these, 470,000 went to the two parts of Palestine not under the control of the Jews: the area that came to be known as the Gaza Strip, in the south of the country, and the area on the West Bank of the River Jordan. Refugee camps were quickly set up in both areas.

Palestinians also fled to neighbouring Arab countries. Lebanon took about 100,000, Syria took 75,000 and Transjordan accepted 70,000. The United Nations soon became involved, and the United Nations Relief and Works Agency (**UNRWA**) was set up to try to provide for the welfare of the refugees. Some of the refugees, especially in Transjordan, moved out of the camps and built a new life in their host countries. But most began a long wait, hoping that one day they could return home.

Arab families during the conflict of 1948, walking from the Haifa area to safety behind the Arab lines in the West Bank.

The Gaza Strip and West Bank quickly came under the control of the Arab states next to them. King Emir Abdullah of Transjordan **annexed** (joined) the West Bank and East Jerusalem to Transjordan. His country changed its name to the '**Hashemite Kingdom of Jordan**'. Egypt controlled the Gaza Strip, but did not make it an official part of Egypt. Its forces, however, remained in the Gaza Strip after the fighting had ended.

In the years since 1948, Palestinians have spread far and wide throughout the Arab world and elsewhere (see pages 28–29). However, many still dream of a time when they will be able to return to the homes they left behind in Palestine.

ARAB ISRAELIS

Some Arabs remained in Israel after 1948, becoming citizens of the new state. By 2004 almost one Israeli in five, over a million of Israel's six million people, was of Arab origin.

A Palestinian Arab woman comforts her son as the turmoil of war swirls around them in 1948.

❝ It should be remembered that the cruelest burden is that borne by the refugees themselves. ❞ (UNRWA's Commissioner General, speaking about the plight of the Palestinian refugees)

Building a Nation

The Jews had created a new country, Israel, and were eager to take their place amongst the other countries of the world. The founders of Israel had always planned that it would be a **democracy**. The first Israeli general election was held in January 1949. Voters chose representatives for the national assembly, known as the **Knesset**.

The first prime minister, David Ben Gurion, was a charismatic figure. Before independence he had led the Jewish Agency, the organization that later became the government. He had also led the Jewish defence force, known as the **Haganah**. The Haganah became the Israeli army after the country gained independence. Ben Gurion served as prime minister between 1948 and 1953, and again from 1955 to 1963.

ISRAEL AND THE USA

Israel benefited from strong support from the USA. The USA was the first country to recognize Israel as a country. In May 1949 US support ensured that Israel became a member of the United Nations.

Israel's first prime minister, David Ben Gurion (wearing a suit), at an independence day parade in 1950.

Israel aimed to create a society where all Jews had an equal chance to live a happy life. The **kibbutz** movement, for example, was an important part of the new society. Kibbutzim were farms where the land and most possessions were shared. At the same time, the cities expanded, and urban life became more comfortable. Life was not good for everyone, however: Arabs who remained in Israeli territory lived under Israeli military rule until 1966.

New Israelis from North Africa arrive at a farming settlement in the northern Israeli region of Galilee.

After independence, the stream of Jewish immigration into Israel became a flood. The Knesset had passed a law called the 'Law of Return'. This said that Jews from anywhere in the world had the right to become Israeli citizens. From 1948 to 1951, 600,000 Jews came to Israel. There were as many new arrivals in three years as there had been in the previous thirty. The new Israelis came from Europe, North and South America and from the Arab world, including Yemen, Iraq, Morocco and elsewhere. Land the Palestinians claimed belonged to them was rapidly filling up with Jewish settlers. Conflict between the two seemed inevitable.

> **❝ Yesterday, for the first time, I was planting potatoes. The rain had stopped and the air smelled good. Never before had I felt so close to my country... ❞**
> (Letter from a young Jewish migrant in Israel)

Wars and their Aftermath: 1956 & 1967

Although the fighting had ended in 1949, Israel and the Arab states were still at war. Fighting would flare up between the two several times over the years to come.

In November 1956, Israel took part in a British and French attack on Egypt. The attack had been caused by a disagreement about the Suez Canal. Israel joined because it claimed it was threatened by Egypt, and because it wanted to be allied to the UK and France. In the end, the attack was a failure.

By 1967 President Gamal Abdul Nasser of Egypt had become a powerful Arab leader. He began to say that the Arabs should attack Israel once more, and reclaim the Palestinians' land. By May of 1967, war seemed imminent. On 5 June 1967, Israel struck first, destroying Egypt's air force. Syria and Jordan joined the battle on the side of Egypt, and fighting raged until 10 June.

" The Israeli Defence Forces have today liberated Jerusalem... We have returned to the most sacred of our shrines, never to part from them again... "
(General Moshe Dayan, Israel's Defence Minister, 7 June 1967)

Israeli armoured vehicles pause as they move through Gaza during the 1967 war.

By the end of the 1967 war, Israel had won an overwhelming victory, taking the **Sinai** Peninsula from the Egyptians, the Golan Heights from Syria and the Jordanian-held West Bank. Israel also captured East Jerusalem, including the Jewish sacred sites there. To the anger of the Arabs, this also meant that Israel now controlled the Muslim and Christian holy places. Finally, the 1967 conflict created 178,000 new Palestinian refugees, while 115,000 Syrians were driven out of the Golan Heights.

Israel returned Sinai to Egypt by 1982, but kept Golan. In the West Bank, Israel wanted to hold on to some territory and return some to Jordan. But Jordan refused to take back only part of its land, so Israel kept it all.

In 1968 the first Israeli settlements in the West Bank were created. Jewish settlers began to move on to what had been Arab land. As the years passed, more and more settlements were built. The Palestinians came to hate and resent Israel even more, as they lost their land and water resources to Jewish settlers.

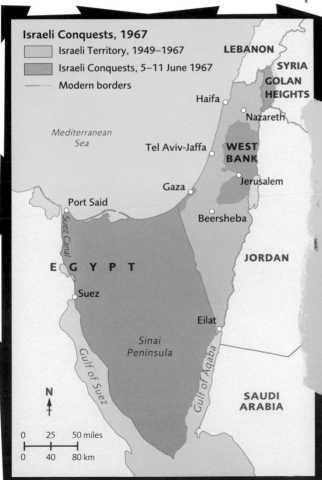

Israeli Conquests, 1967

- Israeli Territory, 1949–1967
- Israeli Conquests, 5–11 June 1967
- ----- Modern borders

LEBANON

SYRIA

GOLAN HEIGHTS

Haifa

Nazareth

Mediterranean Sea

Tel Aviv-Jaffa

WEST BANK

Gaza

Jerusalem

Port Said

Beersheba

Suez Canal

E G Y P T

JORDAN

Suez

Eilat

Sinai Peninsula

Gulf of Suez

Gulf of Aqaba

SAUDI ARABIA

N

0   25   50 miles

0   40   80 km

Israel's territories after the 1967 conflict.

INTERNATIONAL NEGOTIATIONS

In 1967 United Nations Security Council Resolution 242 called on Israel to withdraw from lands captured in 1967, in exchange for peace with the Arab states. Resolution 242 has since been the basis of all discussions over peace between Israel and the Arabs, but there has been endless disagreement about how it can be achieved.

The Palestinians and the PLO

From 1967 the Palestinians who remained in the West Bank and Gaza were under Israeli rule. At first, they accepted their new situation with surprising calm. But inside and outside the West Bank and Gaza, Palestinian opposition to Israel soon began to take shape under the leadership of Yasser Arafat.

Palestinian Fatah guerillas in 2002 celebrate the anniversary of their movement's foundation.

❝ I was impressed by his obvious leadership qualities as I watched him train the men. He was very dynamic, very tough, very passionate. ❞
(Abu Iyad, a founder member of Fatah and one of Yasser Arafat's close friends, speaking about Arafat)

In 1964 a group of exiled Palestinians, encouraged by President Nasser of Egypt, set up the **PLO** (Palestine Liberation Organization). Their aim was to recover Palestine for the Arabs. **Guerrilla** organizations within the PLO were formed, including one called **Fatah**, whose leader was Yasser Arafat. Arafat organized a small group of fighters to attack targets in Israel.

After the Arab defeat in 1967, the PLO began to think that, instead of relying on other countries to help it, the organization should try to recover Palestine by its own actions. This was Yasser Arafat's goal. In 1969 he became Chairman of the PLO's Executive Council, the highest position within the organization. Arafat's Fatah was the most important group within the PLO. The PLO included other institutions representing Palestinian communities abroad and inside Palestine. The most important of these was the Palestine National Council, a kind of parliament where most Palestinian bodies were represented.

The PLO's original aim was to take back the whole of the land of Mandate Palestine, including what was now Israel. The Palestinian National Charter refused to recognize Israel's existence. The Charter said that when Palestinian victory was achieved, however far off that day was, the State of Israel would be abolished, and only a handful of Jews with roots in Palestine would be allowed to remain. This gave Israeli Jews a reason to be seriously worried by the PLO.

YASSER ARAFAT
Arafat was born in 1929 to a family from Gaza, and was brought up in Egypt. He was an engineer by profession, and for many years worked successfully in Kuwait. Arafat quickly rose to the top of the PLO and spent much of his life in exile, in Jordan, Lebanon and Tunisia, travelling the world to raise support for the Palestinians. He eventually returned to Palestine on 1 July 1994, and became president of the Palestinian Authority. He died on 11 November 2004.

The Palestinian leader Yasser Arafat, aged 40. This picture was taken in 1969 while Arafat and the Fatah movement were based in Jordan.

Terrorism as a Weapon

By 1970 the Palestinian guerrilla groups were mainly based in Jordan. The guerrillas began to challenge the authority of King Hussein. Time after time, armed Palestinians clashed with Jordanian troops and police. The guerrillas controlled parts of the country and even some of the capital city, Amman. The Palestinians used Jordan as a base for their attacks on Israel. This led to Israeli revenge attacks on Jordan.

1970: Foreign aircraft were blown up after being hijacked by the Palestinians and brought to Jordan.

On 6 September 1970, the Palestinian guerrillas grabbed the world's attention. They hijacked four international airliners, blowing them up at Dawson's Field, a disused airfield in Jordan. There were no deaths in this incident. After being held for days, 360 passengers and crew were released unharmed. Sixteen Jews among the passengers were held for another month before being released alive.

Yasser Arafat, on 13 December 1988, addressing a special session of the United Nations. In this historic speech, he said the PLO had turned its back on terrorism.

> **Today, I have come bearing an olive branch and a freedom fighter's gun. Do not let the olive branch fall from my hand.**
> *(Yasser Arafat at the UN in 1974)*

King Hussein was furious. He unleashed his army on the Palestinian guerrillas, and drove them out of the country. The Palestinian fighters went to Syria and then to Lebanon. Most ordinary Palestinians in Jordan remained in the country, however, where they now made up at least 50 per cent of the population.

Many Palestinians now believed that terrorism was the best way to attract the attention of the world. In September 1972, at the Munich Olympic Games in West Germany, Palestinian terrorists killed eleven Israeli athletes. The terrorists called themselves Black September, in memory of the Dawson's Field incident.

In November 1974 Yasser Arafat was invited to speak at the United Nations General Assembly in New York. In his speech he seemed to say he would rather negotiate for peace than fight. The PLO was then granted '**Observer Status**' at the United Nations. However Palestinian terrorists continued to carry out attacks. In 1976 a group hijacked an Air France plane in Uganda, but the passengers were rescued by Israeli commandos.

THE ACHILLE LAURO
The last Palestinian hijackings took place in the 1980s. In 1985 the Italian cruise ship *Achille Lauro* was seized in the Mediterranean, and a disabled Jewish-American hostage was thrown overboard. In 1986 another aircraft was hijacked, with the deaths of 20 passengers. In 1988 when Arafat addressed the UN General Assembly again, he gave up terrorism, and accepted Israel's right to exist.

The 1973 Yom Kippur War

In 1970 President Nasser died, and Anwar Sadat became president of Egypt. Sadat was determined to avenge the defeat of 1967, and to place Egypt in a strong position to negotiate peace with Israel. On 6 October 1973, on the Jewish holiday of Yom Kippur, Sadat launched a surprise attack on Israeli forces on the East Bank of the Suez Canal.

The Egyptians recaptured part of the Sinai Peninsula but in an Israeli counter-attack, General Ariel Sharon led a tank attack across the Suez Canal south of the Egyptian positions. The result was military stalemate. Egypt could not take more of Sinai, but the Israelis could not press on with their attack on Egypt. There was also fighting on the Syrian border, though the border between Israeli-held territory and Syria remained virtually the same.

Israeli troops with blindfolded Egyptian soldiers, who were captured in the Israeli counter-attack during the war of 1973.

When the fighting ended, it was clear that the war had not gone well for Israel. Mrs Golda Meir, the prime minister, retired. In a general election in 1977, the Labour Party government was defeated by the Likud Party, led by Menachem Begin. The Likud Party was less interested in making an agreement with the Palestinians than the Labour Party.

The USA helped organize peace negotiations after the 1973 war. It wanted to help the warring parties reach an agreement that would at least avoid further fighting. In the end they met just once, without agreement.

❝ Look, this is the first time that a war between us has ended in equality. We can say we won, and you can say it was a tie. From this position, we can negotiate. This time, we want to end the conflict. ❞
(General Gamasy, Egypt's peace negotiator in 1973, speaking to Israel's General Tal)

Menachem Begin, who was born in Russia, was the first Likud Party prime minister of Israel. He was also the first prime minister who did not come from the Labour Party.

Camp David: Peace Between Israel and Egypt

Egypt's President Sadat believed Israel had wrongly taken the Palestinians' land. But he also thought the time had come to make peace with Israel, and to rid his country of the burden of war.

In 1977 Sadat stunned the world by announcing at very short notice that he intended to fly to Israel to address the Israeli parliament, the Knesset. On 19 November 1977, Israel's Prime Minister Menachem Begin greeted Sadat at Ben Gurion Airport near Tel Aviv. Begin then travelled with the Egyptian leader to Jerusalem, where Sadat made an historic speech to the Knesset.

> **❝ I come to you today in person to build a new life and to establish peace. Imagine with me, a peace agreement in Geneva that we can proclaim to a world thirsting for peace... ❞**
> *(Sadat speaking to the Knesset, November 1977)*

US President Jimmy Carter (centre) with Israel's Prime Minister Menachem Begin (right) and President Sadat of Egypt (left) after signing a peace treaty at Camp David in 1979.

The funeral of Egypt's President Anwar Sadat. He was murdered by Islamic extremists in 1981 while watching a military parade.

Following Sadat's initiative, in September 1978 US President Jimmy Carter invited the two leaders to talks in the USA, at **Camp David** in Maryland. Only the idea that peace was better than war united them. Many arguments between the two sides remained. Over twelve days of sometimes angry talks, an agreement emerged. Egypt was to get back its territory in the Sinai Peninsula, in exchange for making peace.

On 26 March 1979, Egypt and Israel signed a peace treaty. This caused fury in the Arab world, which still did not agree that Israel had the right to exist. The other Arab countries broke off relations with Egypt.

Despite the peace treaty, Israel and Egypt did not become friendly. On 6 October 1981, Sadat was assassinated by Islamic **extremists** who said he had betrayed his country and his religion. By this time, little or no good will remained between Egypt and Israel.

THE PALESTINIANS AND CAMP DAVID

The Palestinians did not benefit from the Camp David talks. Begin had offered them some control over their own areas, but it was very limited. They were no closer to regaining control of Palestine. Many Palestinians thought they had been betrayed by Egypt.

Israel's Lebanon War

On 6 June 1982, Israel invaded Lebanon, its northern neighbour. The operation was planned by Israel's Defence Minister, Ariel Sharon. The declared aim was the creation of a 40-kilometre (25-mile) '**security zone**' in southern Lebanon. This would stop Palestinian guerrillas firing missiles from their bases in Lebanon into Galilee, Israel's northern province.

Menachem Begin (centre) in 1982 with Ariel Sharon (on the left) at Beaufort Castle in southern Lebanon.

ARIEL SHARON, ISRAELI SOLDIER AND POLITICIAN

Born in 1928, Ariel Sharon retired from the Israeli army in 1972. When war broke out in 1973, he was called back to help command the attack on Egypt. Sharon became a member of the Knesset and was a member of Menachem Begin's first government in 1977. He became Israel's prime minister in 2003.

> **❝** It was my Lebanese allies who made me leave Beirut... If I went on fighting, more children would be killed. I felt guilty. **❞**
> *(Yasser Arafat in 1982)*

The Israelis pushed on towards the Lebanese capital, Beirut, where there were more Palestinian fighters. On 1 August 1982, Israeli planes attacked the city. On 12 August US President Ronald Reagan demanded that the fighting should stop. The Palestinian fighters left Lebanon by sea, heading for Tunisia and Yemen. A multinational force from Europe and the USA oversaw the evacuation.

The aftermath of Israeli bombing raids on Beirut. The Israeli planes were trying to destroy Palestinian strongholds.

At the time there was a civil war inside Lebanon, with local Muslims and the Palestinians fighting Lebanese Christians. Lebanon's President Bashir Gemayel was a Christian. On 14 September Gemayel was assassinated. Some Christians wanted revenge. On 16 September some of Gemayel's supporters entered two Palestinian refugee camps. They spent the next two days killing Palestinians. Israel was blamed for allowing the murderers access to the camps, then not stopping the killings.

In late September Israeli forces began to withdraw from Lebanon. At home in Israel, public opinion was deeply divided about the Lebanese attack. Many said it was not Israel's business to interfere in neighbouring countries. Ariel Sharon resigned as defence minister after official criticism that, as the person in overall charge of the operation, he had not acted correctly. However, Israel continued to occupy part of southern Lebanon until 2000.

Palestinians Around the World

In 1988 the United Nations counted the Palestinian refugees. By this time 381,000 Palestinian refugees lived in camps in the West Bank (alongside the Palestinian population already settled there) and 453,000 in the Gaza Strip. The Palestinian refugee population of Jordan was 862,000. Lebanon had 286,000; Syria had 263,000. This made a total of 2,245,000 people.

Some Palestinians no longer lived in refugee camps. Instead they had left the camps and become part of the local population. No accurate count exists of Palestinians who do not register themselves as refugees, but by 1988

PALESTINIANS IN THE WEST

Estimates suggest that up to 150,000 Palestinians moved to the USA, 100,000 to Europe and smaller numbers to Australia and Latin America. Many of the descendants of these Palestinians have now become citizens of their new countries.

The Shuafat refugee camp near Jerusalem. There are no proper roads or sewers, and children play around uncollected rubbish.

Employees of UNRWA unload sacks of flour at Jabalaya refugee camp in Gaza. UNRWA is the main employer in Gaza, as well as providing aid.

> **ÇÇ As Palestinians, we grieve for what we have lost, and few people have lost more than us. But grief can be made less by the fellowship of friends. ϑϑ**
> (A Palestinian Christian woman)

there were up to a million in Jordan, where they were able to become citizens. Citizenship helped many refugees begin to lead normal lives in their new country. However, tens of thousands of Palestinians in Syria and in Lebanon continued to live in very poor camps, which were very hard to leave.

There were also Palestinians in other Arab countries, and in the West. But however long a Palestinian doctor or accountant might live in Kuwait or New York, he or she never forgot their Palestinian roots.

In the refugee camps of the West Bank, Jordan and Lebanon, the ordinary Palestinians never stopped thinking of returning to the lands and homes they had left. Most, though, probably knew that being able to return to Israel was unlikely. Much of the land they had left behind was now occupied by Israelis, who would not make way for a Palestinian return.

A Decade of Change: Israel in the 1980s

When the Likud government came to power in 1977, there were just 30 Jewish settlements in the West Bank, inhabited by about 4,500 people. They were there because Israel wanted to safeguard the border between the West Bank and Israel, and to control the border with Jordan. Another 50,000 Israelis lived in the area around East Jerusalem that had been taken over by Israel.

❝ Our aim is to bring about ... the fulfilment of the Zionist vision in its full scope. ❞
(Gush Emunim statement justifying their plan to build settlements everywhere in the West Bank and Gaza, thus putting Jews in every part of Palestine)

This photo shows buildings being constructed for Jewish people in the mainly Arab West Bank town of Hebron in 1988.

From 1977 onwards, more settlements appeared. The Israeli government encouraged Jewish settlers to move into the West Bank. By the end of the 1980s, there were almost 100,000 settlers in the West Bank, with a few thousand in Gaza, and well over 120,000 in East Jerusalem. Water is precious in the dry lands of the Middle East, and Israel also took control of the main water sources in the West Bank.

Many of the settlers were American Jews belonging to a religious group called Gush Emunim, which in Hebrew means 'The Bloc of the Faithful'. The religious settlers said that it was their duty to resettle the lands of ancient Israel. Other settlers moved for the cheap land and houses. After 1991 some settlers were Russian Jews, who had begun to arrive in Israel.

In Israel the 1980s were marked by political uncertainty. New political forces emerged, including religious political parties such as **Shas**. Neither Labour nor Likud was able to completely win an election. Instead there was a series of 'national governments' in which they shared power.

An armed Israeli settler walks through the streets of Hebron.

THE SHAS PARTY

Shas was founded in the 1980s as a religious party for Jews of Eastern origin, for example, from Arab countries such as Iraq, Syria, Yemen, Egypt, Tunisia and Morocco. Jews also came from further afield, for example, from India and Iran. A key figure in the movement was Rabbi Ovadia Yosef.

The First Intifada

On 8 December 1987, Israeli troops and Palestinians clashed in the West Bank when an Israeli truck hit a car in Gaza, killing four civilians. A Palestinian protest began, which the Palestinians called the *intifada*. This is an Arab word that means 'shaking off'.

For the first time, stones were thrown at Israeli troops. Three days later, in the West Bank, Israeli soldiers fired at a crowd, killing a girl. By the end of January 1988, 42 Palestinians had been killed, and by September, the number had risen to 346. But the intifada showed no sign of ending.

ROOTS OF THE INTIFADA

The intifada happened as the Palestinians became more and more eager to have their own country. In November 1988 Yasser Arafat actually declared the existence of a Palestinian state. However, few of the world's countries agreed that this new country really existed.

Palestinian youths throw stones at Israeli troops towards the end of the first intifada.

Secret local committees, including PLO members, organized the intifada. Palestinian workers' strikes began, causing problems for Israel, which had become dependent on Palestinian workers.

At first Israel tried to arrest the ringleaders, but that made the demonstrations grow stronger. Israel lost world sympathy, as stone-throwing demonstrators faced armed soldiers on the nightly TV news. The treatment of Palestinian Muslims influenced the attitude of Muslims all around the world. Many of them began to oppose Israel and the USA, which they thought supported Israel rather than the Palestinians.

Eventually, the intifada slowed down. The world's attention was gripped by the Gulf crisis of 1990–1991. Many Palestinians admired Saddam Hussein because of his strong stance against Israel, so the PLO supported his invasion of Kuwait. This lost them much world sympathy. Behind the scenes, moves towards peace between Israel and the Palestinians were already under way. By 1993 the first intifada had almost ended.

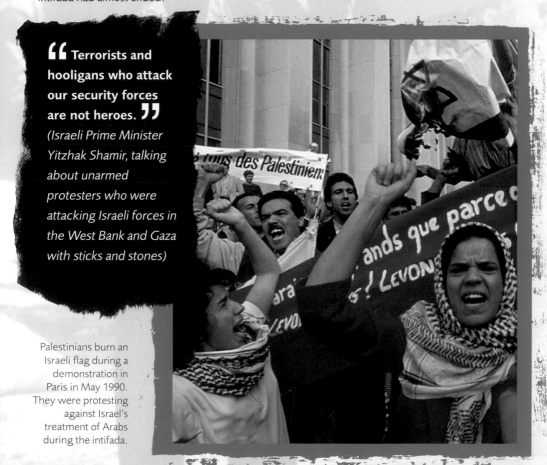

ff Terrorists and hooligans who attack our security forces are not heroes. JJ
(Israeli Prime Minister Yitzhak Shamir, talking about unarmed protesters who were attacking Israeli forces in the West Bank and Gaza with sticks and stones)

Palestinians burn an Israeli flag during a demonstration in Paris in May 1990. They were protesting against Israel's treatment of Arabs during the intifada.

Thoughts of Peace

Once the Gulf War was over, US President George H. W. Bush judged that the moment had come to try to end the hostility between Israel and the Arabs, which had lasted since 1948. In October 1991, he hosted a conference in the Spanish capital, Madrid. Attended by Israel and several Arab states, it was the first Middle East peace conference since 1973.

President Gorbachev of the former Soviet Union, Spanish Prime Minister Felipe Gonzalez, and US President George H. W. Bush with other world leaders at the Madrid peace conference in 1991.

❝ What we want to see is a Middle East no longer victimized by fear and terror, where men and women lead normal lives. ❞
(US President George H. W. Bush, Madrid, October 1991)

The USA used all its authority and influence to bring the parties to the table. For the first time a Palestinian delegation met the Israelis face to face. (At the opening sessions, the Palestinians were there as part of the Jordanian delegation.) The moment seemed to signal a real change, though Israel's hard-line government, led by Yitzhak Shamir, seemed unwilling to give much away.

After Madrid the Israelis and Palestinians met in eleven further sessions of talks in Washington over a year and a half. A Labour-led government took over in Israel in July 1992. But hopes of a change in attitude seemed to fade in December 1992, when Israel's Prime Minister Yitzhak Rabin deported 400 activists of **Hamas**, one of the Palestinian extremist movements that had formed among the Palestinians.

Meanwhile in the USA, President Clinton took over from President Bush in January 1993. The Palestinians feared Clinton might be less sympathetic towards them, but he seemed committed to the search for Middle East peace. In 1993 the USA decided to take an active part in the talks instead of being only an observer.

More than 400 Palestinians were deported by Israel in December 1992 because of their links to Hamas.

The Oslo Accords

Both Israel and the Palestinians wanted peace, but feared the official talks in Washington were going nowhere. In December 1992 secret talks began with help from the Norwegian foreign ministry. This happened as the eighth round of official talks was taking place in Washington.

From January 1993 Israeli and Palestinian **negotiators** met in secret in Oslo, Norway's capital. The Israeli negotiators were at first not directly connected with the government. The leading Palestinian negotiator was Ahmed Qureia, known as Abu Ala, who was a senior figure in the PLO. (In September 2003 Qureia became prime minister of the Palestinian Authority.) From May 1993 the Israeli team of negotiators was led by a diplomat, Uri Savir.

OSLO ACCORDS

'The government of the State of Israel and the ... Jordanian-Palestinian delegation agree that it is time to put an end to decades of confrontation and conflict ... and strive to live in peaceful coexistence.'
(Opening text of the Declaration of Principles on Interim Self-Government Arrangements, part of the Oslo Accords)

Hosted by US President Clinton, Israeli Prime Minister Yitzhak Rabin (left) shakes hands with Yasser Arafat (right), after signing the peace agreement between Israel and the PLO.

An agreement was signed on 20 August 1993, while the Israeli foreign minister Shimon Peres was visiting Norway. The Palestinians hoped it would allow them to govern themselves in Palestine. The agreement said that after **permanent status talks** the Palestinians would get their 'legitimate rights', which they took to mean statehood. Most of the really difficult points, like the future of Jerusalem and the settlements, and the claims of refugees, were left to be dealt with at the permanent status talks.

Palestinians in Gaza celebrate the signing of the Palestinian-Israeli peace accords.

Not everyone was pleased with the Oslo Accord. The Likud opposition in Israel was unhappy with the agreement, while many Palestinians feared that too much had been given away. On 13 September 1993, a ceremony to finalize the accord was held in Washington, D.C., on the White House lawn. As a result, in October 1994, the Hashemite Kingdom of Jordan made peace with Israel, after being at war since 1948.

> **❝ The Palestinians have given away virtually everything in exchange for very little. ❞**
> *(Edward Said, Palestinian intellectual and professor at Columbia University in New York)*

The 1990s: A Decade of Disappointment

Israel's Prime Minister Yitzhak Rabin (far right) visits with Israel's Arabic-speaking community.

The details of the way forward from the Oslo agreement proved very difficult to agree, and many sessions of talks were held.

The first result of these talks was that the Palestinians were given some control over Gaza and Jericho. Then, in September 1995, it was agreed that the Palestinians would also get some control over the West Bank. The West Bank was divided into three areas. Israel would withdraw completely from the places where most Palestinians lived, but would continue to protect its settlers in other parts, while holding onto still more territory for 'security reasons'.

YITZHAK RABIN

Yitzhak Rabin was born in Jerusalem in 1922. He served in the Israeli army for 27 years, and was then Israeli ambassador in the USA. In 1974 he became prime minister for the first time. He was minister of defence from 1984 to 1990, then became prime minister again in 1992. He was known as a Labour 'hawk'. His tough approach meant that the Israeli people trusted him to make peace.

In the mid-1990s, extremist Palestinian organizations including **Palestinian Jihad** and Hamas had become more important. These groups claimed to be based on the Islamic faith. They rejected the peace process, and began to use suicide bombing as a weapon. More than 70 Israelis were killed in the first year after suicide bombing began in April 1994.

In November 1995 the Israeli Prime Minister Yitzhak Rabin was murdered by a **right-wing** Israeli extremist. The situation in Israel became tense, but the peace process went on, and a Palestinian Council was elected. At the Israeli elections in May 1996, the Labour government lost power. Likud leader Binyamin Netanyahu was elected as prime minister.

> **We want to make sure that we maintain the momentum towards peace, that we help the parties hold onto the gains that they've made, and that we continue down the road.**
> *(Former US Secretary of State Warren Christopher)*

The scene of a suicide bombing in Jerusalem in 1996. A bus has been blown up by a Palestinian suicide bomber.

The 'Best Offer'

Prime Minister Netanyahu's strategy was to try to make a final peace with the Palestinians, with everything agreed at once. In October 1998 he agreed with Yasser Arafat to reopen negotiations on the future of the Palestinians. In return, Arafat was expected to clamp down on Palestinian violence.

Netanyahu lost an election on 18 May 1999. Ehud Barak, another Labour hawk, became the new prime minister of Israel. Barak was determined to make a final effort to come to a real agreement with the Palestinians, and Israeli voters showed their approval by voting for him. A round of talks, known as Camp David II, began in the summer of 2000.

US President Clinton looks on in July 2000 as Yasser Arafat and Prime Minister Ehud Barak shake hands.

In December 2000 Barak made what he claimed was an extremely generous offer to Arafat. Barak claimed his offer included 95 per cent of the West Bank, but the Palestinians said this was only after 20 per cent had already been taken away for Israeli settlements and security zones. What was left was less than 80 per cent of the West Bank, divided up by Israeli roads. The Palestinians said they were offered only limited rights in Jerusalem, and Arafat was asked to agree that no Palestinian refugees would have the right to return to their original homes, which were now in Israel. Finally Israel was set to keep key West Bank water sources. In the end the Palestinians decided to reject Barak's offer.

> **❝ If peace talks fail, this will endanger the security of Israel's citizens, and also Israel's future as a Jewish and democratic state. ❞**
> *(Ehud Barak)*

A FINAL, FINAL OFFER

At talks in Taba, Egypt, in January 2001, Israeli Prime Minister Ehud Barak made an improved peace offer. But the offer came too late: Barak's political career was coming to an end (see pages 42–43). In February 2001 he lost the election for the post of prime minister, and the Taba offer was withdrawn.

Below left: Barak's 'Best Offer' of December 2000.

Below right: The improved offer made at the Taba talks in January 2001.

Barak's Offer, December 2000

☐ Palestinian control
▨ Retained by Israel

WEST BANK

Dead Sea

N

0   5   10   15   20 miles
0   8   16   24   32 km

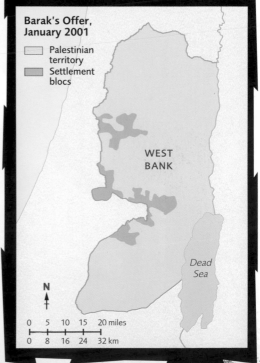

Barak's Offer, January 2001

☐ Palestinian territory
▨ Settlement blocs

WEST BANK

Dead Sea

N

0   5   10   15   20 miles
0   8   16   24   32 km

From Barak to Sharon

The Al-Aqsa Intifada started on 29 September 2000, and caused fear and anger in Israel. Endless demonstrations were accompanied by violence by the Palestinians. The Israeli security forces struck back, killing many Palestinians.

According to Palestinian sources, almost 3,000 people had been killed in Israeli attacks on Palestinian targets by March 2004. Eighty per cent of these were said to be civilians rather than fighters. By April 2004, 972 Israelis had died, of whom 295 were soldiers.

> **Lip service [talk] doesn't make peace. What is needed is to end the Israeli military deployment in the West Bank and Gaza.**
> (Saeb Erakat, the senior Palestinian peace negotiator)

Palestinian youths flee as shots ring out in Ramallah in October 2000.

> **" If the Palestinians choose the path of peace … they will find me and my government a sincere and true partner. "**
> *(Ariel Sharon)*

In February 2001, amid a continually troubled atmosphere in Israel, Barak lost his bid for a second term as prime minister. His successor was Israel's toughest right-wing politician, the Likud leader Ariel Sharon. Sharon said he was willing to compromise with the Palestinians, but he would not talk under what he called 'the pressure of violence and terror'. He also said that the Oslo peace process was of no more use in finding a way to peace.

On 24 June 2002, President George W. Bush made a speech saying that Israel should settle all issues with the Palestinians, in exchange for peace. In April 2003 the US plan was set out in a proposal known as the '**Road Map**'.

On 4 June 2003, the Road Map was accepted by all the parties at a summit meeting held at Aqaba in Jordan, attended by President George W. Bush, Jordan's King Abdullah, Ariel Sharon and the new Palestinian prime minister, Mahmoud Abbas.

The Road Map asked both sides for difficult things. Israel did not want to stop building settlements, and the Palestinian Authority was unable to stop the violence. By 2004 the Road Map seemed virtually dead. Israel had had enough of the violence and bombings. Meanwhile daily life had become next to impossible for the Palestinians, in the face of Israeli road blocks and raids. To both sides peace seemed as far away as ever.

From left to right: the then Palestinian prime minister (and later president), Mahmoud Abbas, US president George W. Bush and Israeli prime minister Ariel Sharon attend a meeting in Jordan in June 2003.

THE ROAD MAP

In 2002 an international group was set up to supervise peace plans. The plans included the end of violence on the part of the Palestinians, and a complete halt to further building or expansion of settlements by Israel. Neither of these have been carried out.

The Issues

In addition to viewing each other with great hostility, Israel and the Palestinians struggle because they disagree over many issues related to their rights and the ownership of resources.

First there is the question of statehood, or the right to be a nation. Palestine was divided into two parts by the United Nations, but Israel has become a country, while Palestine has not. Some say this is the fault of the Palestinians. Whether this is so or not, almost 70 years after the UN partition, the Palestinians still have no country.

Then there is the issue of refugees. Many Palestinians left their country when Israel was established in 1948. Israel will not allow the return of Palestinians who left, and this means they cannot go back to their homes.

> ❝ Let us pray for all the victims of this violence, for their families, for the people who still live in shock and fear. Let us hope and pray that anger will not result in hate or revenge. ❞
> *(A prayer from the World Council of Churches, meeting in Jerusalem)*

A Palestinian man tends his sheep on a hillside opposite the Israeli settlement of Maale Adumim in the West Bank, near Jerusalem.

The Palestinians also feel bitter about the Israeli settlements. They do not want the Israelis who have come to live in the West Bank and Gaza, the part of Palestine that was theirs before 1967, to remain there. In addition, Palestinian Muslims and Christians feel they are denied their rights in Jerusalem, a holy city for them, as well as the Jews. Israel, though, claims it will never give up its access to the Western Wall in Jerusalem, the holiest place of all for Jews.

THE 'SECURITY FENCE'

In 2002 Israel began building a wall around the West Bank, in places cutting deep into occupied Palestinian territory. The Palestinians claim the fence is another Israeli attempt to seize more of their territory, and will ruin the lives of thousands of Palestinians living nearby. The Israelis, on the other hand, claim that the fence is the only way they can protect their cities from the menace of more suicide bombers.

Finally, for the Israelis, the greatest problem of all is security. Israel has always feared it could be destroyed by Arab invaders, and this is why military strength is a key issue in the country. Now it fears slow destruction from the inside by Palestinian violence.

A Palestinian family walks along the security fence, a concrete barrier blocking the road between Jerusalem and the West Bank.

Looking Towards the Future

On 11 November 2004, the veteran Palestinian leader Yasser Arafat died at the age of 75. Many Palestinians mourned their leader. Israel took the view that with Yasser Arafat gone, there could be a chance to solve the Middle East conflict.

Arafat had made the world aware of the Palestine problem, and he had led the Palestinians through difficult times. It was also Arafat who led the Palestinians in triumph when he returned in 1994 to be president of the Palestinian Authority.

" Israel is becoming a graveyard of children. The Holy Land is being turned into a wasteland. If an Israeli child is killed and the next day a Palestinian child is killed, it's no solution. "
(Nurit and Rami Elhanan, Israelis whose 14-year-old daughter died in a suicide bomb attack)

At a rally on 15 May 2004, tens of thousands of Israelis called for Ariel Sharon to withdraw Israeli settlers and troops from Gaza.

A Jewish settler and his daughter take cover from Palestinian gunfire as Palestinians attack a memorial service at a settlement in Gaza.

THE NEED FOR COMPROMISE

The problem in the future, as in the past, will be to find areas of compromise between Israelis and Palestinians. Extremists on both sides have a lot of influence. Ariel Sharon's hard-line supporters are not eager to pull out of any Israeli-held territory. The Palestinians dislike the idea of agreeing that any settlements will remain. The extremists will have to be persuaded to abandon violence.

Many Palestinians believed it was only through Arafat's leadership that they might eventually have a state of their own.

After Arafat's death, the leaders of the Palestinian Authority moved quickly to put a new leader in place. Mahmoud Abbas, who had been prime minister in 2003, became chairman of the Palestine Liberation Organization. He was also elected president of the Palestinian Authority.

The Israeli leadership had always viewed Arafat with distrust, and did not conceal their relief that he had left the scene. In particular Prime Minister Ariel Sharon had always hated Arafat. The Israelis quickly said that the existence of a new Palestinian leadership gave an ideal opportunity for a new approach to peace. In 2005, they promised to withdraw their settlements and troops completely from the Gaza Strip.

However, by the middle of 2005, there was still no sign that Israel and the Palestinians would be able to make a permanent agreement for the future.

Glossary

Al-Aqsa Intifada violence that broke out in Palestine in September 2000. The word *intifada* means 'shaking off' in Arabic.

annex, annexation take something for yourself, and to attach it to what you already have

Balfour Declaration important letter written in 1917 by the British Foreign Secretary, Arthur Balfour, saying that Great Britain would accept Jewish immigration into Palestine

Camp David place in the US state of Maryland for the president of the USA to relax and entertain. It is also used as the location for many important international meetings.

democracy system in which the people of a country hold elections to choose who their government leaders will be. In a democratic country, there is also what is known as the rule of law. This means the government cannot do what it likes, but must obey the law.

extremist someone who uses forceful actions to create political change. Some extremists believe that any action, even murder, is acceptable in the name of their beliefs.

Fatah Palestinian National Liberation Movement founded in the early 1960s by Yasser Arafat. It is the most important group in the Palestinian Liberation Organization.

guerrilla person who fights in small independent groups, usually not in uniform

Haganah Jewish Defence Force in Palestine before 1948. It became the Israeli Defence Force (the Israeli Army) after the declaration of the State of Israel.

Hamas Islamic Resistance Movement formed in 1987. It is both a political and militant organization operating in the Israeli-occupied West Bank and the Gaza Strip. The USA, Israel and the European Union all regard it as a terrorist organization.

Hashemite Kingdom of Jordan name given to Jordan by King Adbullah I, the first King, in honour of his family, known in the Middle East as the Hashemites

hawk, hawkish 'hawks' take a tough line in politics

Holocaust Nazi Germany's systematic genocide of Jews and other ethnic and social groups during World War II, starting in 1941 and continuing through to 1945. Six million Jews and millions of other peoples were killed during the Holocaust.

kibbutz, kibbutzim in Israel, a kibbutz is a farm run by a group, where there is no private property. *Kibbutzim* means more than one kibbutz.

Knesset Israeli parliament

League of Nations international body set up after the end of World War I. It stopped working effectively in the 1930s, but inspired the United Nations.

mandate arrangement where a developed country became a kind of caretaker, looking after a new country until it was ready for independence

negotiator person who helps groups who disagree to reach some sort of settlement or agreement. Governments and nations with opposing views sometimes need negotiators to come to agreements.

Observer Status at an international organization, Observer Status means being present at meetings without speaking or voting

Ottoman Empire great international empire in the Middle East, governed by the Turks. The empire lasted from the 16th century until World War I.

Palestinian Authority governs parts of the West Bank and the Gaza Strip. It was established as a result of the Oslo accords between the PLO and Israel. The Palestinian Authority has control over both security-related and civilian issues in Palestinian urban areas (called in the Oslo accords 'Area A'), and civilian control over Palestinian rural areas ('Area B').

Palestinian Jihad militant group, widely regarded as a terrorist group. Its goal is the destruction of the State of Israel and its replacement with an Islamist state for Palestinian Arabs.

permanent status talks talks to decide what the final solution to the Israel-Palestine conflict will be

PLO (Palestine Liberation Organization) founded in 1964 as a Palestinian nationalist organization dedicated to the establishment of an independent Palestinian state. In 1969 Arafat became chairman of the PLO's Executive Committee, a position he held until his death in 2004.

right-wing describes a person or party that has very conservative political views. The opposite is left-wing, with very liberal views.

Road Map plan to resolve the Israeli-Palestinian conflict proposed by the USA, the European Union, Russia and the United Nations. The principles of the plan were first outlined by US President George W. Bush in a speech on 24 June 2002, in which he called for an independent Palestinian state living side by side with the Israeli state, in peace.

Security Council decision-making body at the United Nations. It consists of 15 members, 5 of them permanent (the UK, the USA, France, Russia and China).

security zone strip of land occupied by the Israelis in Lebanon between 1982 and 2000, intended to keep the enemy at a distance

Shas Party religious party set up for Jews of Middle Eastern, North African and Asian origin. It is the third strongest party in the Israeli Knesset.

Sinai peninsula of Egyptian territory between Egypt proper and Palestine

Temple Mount what remains of the ancient Jewish temple in Jerusalem, upon which two mosques are now built. Jews pray at the 'Western Wall', next to the Temple Mount.

United Nations (UN) international body created in 1945, after World War II, to safeguard world peace

UNRWA United Nations Relief and Works Agency, set up in 1949 to assist the Palestinian refugees

World War I First World War, from 1914 to 1918, when Great Britain, France and the USA fought Germany, Austria and the Ottoman Empire (with many other countries joining in on each side). Britain, France and the USA were the victors.

World War II Second World War, from 1939 to 1945, when the UK, France and the USA fought Germany, Italy and Japan, again with many other countries involved. The USA and the UK were once more the victors, and set up the United Nations after the war was over.

Zionist movement Zionism is at the heart of the Zionist movement. It is the belief held by some Jews that the Jewish people must have a country of their own to live in and a state of their own to govern them.

Facts and Figures

ISRAEL
Area: 20,770 square kilometres (8,000 sq mi)
Population: 6,276,883
0–14 years   27%
15–64 years   63%
65 years and over   10%
Population growth rate: 1.2%
Life expectancy at birth: 79 years
Religions:
Jewish   80%
Muslim   15%
Christian   2%
Other   3%
Literacy rate: 95%
GDP per capita: US$20,800
Unemployment rate: 10.7%

THE WEST BANK
Area: 5,860 square kilometres (2,260 sq mi)
Population: 2,385,615
0–14 years   44%
15–64 years   53%
65 years and over   3%
Jewish settlers: 187,000
Population growth rate: 3.2%
Life expectancy at birth: 73 years
Religions:
Muslim   75%
Jewish (in settlements)   17%
Christian (mainly Arabs)   8%
Literacy rate: Unknown
GDP per capita: US$800
Unemployment rate: 50%

THE GAZA STRIP
Area: 360 square kilometres (140 sq mi)
Population: 1,376,289
0–14 years   48%
15–64 years   49%
65 years and over   3%
Jewish settlers: 5,000
Population growth rate: 3.7%
Life expectancy at birth: 72 years
Religions:
Muslim   98.7%
Christian   0.7%
Jewish (in settlements)   0.6%
Literacy rate: Unknown
GDP per capita: US$600
Unemployment rate: 50%

(Source: CIA World Factbook, 2005)*

PALESTINIAN POPULATION REGISTERED WITH UNRWA AS REFUGEES

	Registered as refugees	Resident in refugee camps
West Bank	655,000	177,000
Gaza	907,000	479,000
Jordan	1,719,000	304,000
Syria	410,000	120,000
Lebanon	392,000	222,000
TOTAL:	**4,083,000**	**1,302,000**

WORLD PALESTINIAN POPULATION (OUTSIDE ISRAEL/WEST BANK/GAZA)

Country/Region	Population
Jordan	2,598,000
Lebanon	388,000
Syria	395,000
Saudi Arabia	287,000
Gulf States	152,000
Egypt	58,000
Other Arab States	113,000
North & South America	216,000
Other countries	275,000
TOTAL	**4,482,000**

WORLD TOTAL PALESTINIAN POPULATION *(including residents in Israel, residents in the West Bank and Gaza, refugees and expatriates and their descendants regarding themselves as Palestinians)*

TOTAL	**8,852,574**

(Source: estimates based on figures for 2001– 2003 from PASSIA, the Palestinian Academic Society for the Study of International Affairs)

Timelines

LONG LINE

61 BCE	Roman conquest of Jerusalem
40 BCE	Herod the Great comes to the throne
4 BCE	Historical date of birth of Jesus
70 CE	First Jewish Revolt
73 CE	The fall of the Temple to the Romans
133 CE	Second Jewish Revolt
313 CE	Roman Emperor Constantine legalizes Christian faith
610 CE	The Prophet Mohammed founds Islam
632 CE	Arab conquest of Jerusalem
715 CE	The present Al-Aqsa Mosque is built
1099 CE	Crusaders conquer Jerusalem
1291	Crusaders driven out of Palestine
1517	Ottoman Turks conquer Jerusalem
1878	Earliest Zionist settlement in Palestine
1909	Zionist immigrants found city of Tel Aviv

Scale (left axis): 100 BCE, 0, 100 CE, 200 CE, 300 CE, 400 CE, 500 CE, 600 CE, 700 CE, 800 CE, 900 CE, 1000 CE, 1100 CE, 1200 CE, 1300 CE, 1400 CE, 1500 CE, 1600 CE, 1700 CE, 1800 CE, 1900 CE, 2000 CE

20TH AND 21ST CENTURY LINE

1917	The Balfour Declaration
1922	Start of the British Mandate
1936	The Arab revolt
1948	End of the British Mandate
1948	Israel's War of Independence
1948	Founding of the State of Israel
1949	Armistice agreements signed
1956	Suez Campaign
1964	PLO (Palestine Liberation Organization) founded
1967	June War between Israel and the Arabs
1973	Yom Kippur War between Israel and the Arabs
1979	Israel and Egypt sign Peace Treaty Sinai is returned to Egypt
1987	First Palestinian uprising, or 'Intifada', begins
1993	Oslo Declaration
1995	Interim agreement (Oslo II)
2000	Al-Aqsa Intifada begins
2002	Sharon government begins to build security fence
2003	US Road Map plan is drawn up
2004	Yasser Arafat dies
2005	Mahmoud Abbas elected president of Palestinian Authority

Scale (right axis): 1910, 1920, 1930, 1940, 1950, 1960, 1970, 1980, 1990, 2000, 2005

Who's Who?

Abbas, Mahmoud (Abu Mazen) Abbas was born in 1935 in Safed, now in Israel. He became a refugee in 1948, fleeing with his family to Syria. He studied in Damascus and the Soviet Union, and joined Fatah in 1959. He remained close to Arafat and became the PLO's 'foreign minister'. He supervised the 1993 Oslo talks. In 2003 Abbas was briefly appointed Palestinian prime minister. Abbas was elected president of the Palestinian Authority in succession to Yasser Arafat in 2005.

Abdullah I (Emir Abdullah) King of Jordan. One of the sons of Sherif Hussein of Mecca, who led the Arab Revolt against the Ottoman Empire in World War I. After the Allied victory in World War I, Great Britain was effectively in control of the Middle East and was awarded the League of Nations Mandate over Palestine. The British made Abdullah the Emir of Transjordan, the eastern part of the Palestine Mandate. He later became King when Transjordan became the independent Kingdom of Jordan.

Arafat, Yasser (Abu Ammar) Arafat claimed to have been born in Jerusalem in 1929, but spent much of his childhood and youth in Cairo, Egypt. He was a founder member of the anti-Israel guerrilla movement Fatah in around 1959, and was chairman of the PLO (Palestine Liberation Organization) from 1969. Arafat signed the Oslo peace accords with Israel in 1993, and became president of the Palestinian Authority in 1996. He died in 2004.

Balfour, Arthur Balfour was the foreign minister of Great Britain in 1917. He had earlier served as prime minister. He drafted the so-called 'Balfour Declaration', in the form of a letter to the Zionist leader Lord Rothschild. In this letter he promised the Jews what he called a 'national home in Palestine'. The result was that the British administration later allowed Jewish immigration into Palestine, helping Israel to become a country.

Barak, Ehud Barak was born in Palestine in 1942. He became chief of staff in 1994. He was a professional soldier until 1996. Barak was elected to the Knesset in 1996, and served as Labour prime minister from 1999 to 2001.

Begin, Menachem Begin was born in Brest-Litovsk (then in Russia) in 1913, and died in 1992. He moved to Palestine in 1943. From 1948 to 1977, he led the Likud Party. In 1977 he became the first Likud prime minister. He signed Israel's peace treaty with Egypt in 1979. Begin resigned and left politics in 1983.

Ben Gurion, David Ben Gurion was Israel's first prime minister. He was born in what is now Poland in 1886, and died in 1973. He moved to Palestine in 1906. Ben Gurion was prime minister of Israel from 1948 to 1953 and from 1955 to 1963.

Bush, George H. W. 41st president of the USA (1989–1993). Bush was born in 1924. He arranged the Madrid Middle East Peace conference of 1991.

Bush, George W. 43rd president of the USA (2001–due to leave office in 2009). Bush was born in 1946. In 2002 he set up the 'Quartet' group (the USA, Russia, the UN and the European Union), which produced the 'Road Map' for Middle East peace.

Carter, James E. (Jimmy) 39th president of the USA (1977–1981). Carter was born in 1924. He oversaw the peace talks between Egypt and Israel that led to the peace treaty of 1979.

Clinton, William (Bill) 42nd president of the USA (1993–2001). Clinton was born in 1946. He attempted to reach a Middle East peace settlement in 2000/2001.

Dayan, Moshe Dayan was born in Palestine in 1915 and died in 1981. He fought in Israel's War of Independence in 1948. He was army chief of staff from 1953. Dayan was elected to the Knesset as a Labour member in 1959, and held ministerial posts including minister of defence and foreign minister.

Eisenhower, Dwight D. 34th president of the USA (1953–1961). He was born in 1890, and died in 1969. He announced the 'Eisenhower doctrine' that the USA would intervene to block the expansion of communism anywhere in the world.

Gemayel, Bashir President Gemayel of Lebanon, a Maronite Christian, was born in 1947. He was the son of Pierre Gemayel, a veteran Lebanese politician and head of the right-wing Christian Kata'ib Party. He led the Kata'ib's military wing in the Lebanese civil war. He became president of Lebanon in 1982, but was murdered a few weeks later.

Hussein King Hussein of Jordan was the grandson of King Abdullah I. He became King of Jordan in 1953 at the age of 18. He lived until 1999, and played a large role in peace negotiations in the Middle East.

Nasser, Gamal Abdul President Nasser of Egypt was born in 1918 and died in 1970. As a young officer, he was the leader of the Egyptian Revolution in 1952, and took the title of president in 1954. He led the Arabs in the war against Israel in 1967, and offered to resign after the war was lost. He died of heart disease in 1970.

Netanyahu, Binyamin Netanyahu was born in Tel Aviv in 1949. He served in the Israeli forces, and became an anti-terrorism specialist. Netanyahu joined the Israeli embassy in the USA in 1982. He was elected to the Knesset in 1988. Netanyahu became prime minister in 1996, and resigned in 1999. He has been minister of foreign affairs since 2002.

Peres, Shimon Peres was born in Belarus in 1923, and moved to Palestine in 1934. He is a former soldier and diplomat. He joined the Knesset in 1959. Peres has held numerous posts as minister and several times served as prime minister of Israel. He became deputy prime minister in January 2005.

Qureia, Ahmed (Abu Ala) Qureia was born in 1937 in Abu Dis, in the West Bank, near Jerusalem. His father was a wealthy businessman. Queria became a banker. He joined Fatah in 1968, and started to run the PLO's investment and economics department from 1970. He then became the PLO's 'economics minister'. Qureia became close to Yasser Arafat, then joined the Fatah central committee in 1989. In 1993 he played a leading role as a negotiator in the Oslo talks. He became speaker of the Palestinian Legislative Council (Parliament) in 1996. Qureia became the Palestinian prime minister in 2003.

Rabin, Yitzhak Rabin was born in Jerusalem in 1922, and murdered in 1995. He was elected to the Knesset as a Labour Party member in 1973. He served as an army general, a minister and twice as prime minister, with the second occasion from 1992 until his death. Rabin signed the peace agreement with the Palestinians in 1993.

Reagan, Ronald 40th president of the USA (1981–1989). Reagan was born in 1911, and died in 2004. In 1982 he announced the Reagan Plan for Middle East peace.

Sadat, Anwar President Sadat of Egypt, Nasser's successor, was born in 1918. He was part of the group of officers led by Nasser who started the Egyptian Revolution in 1952. He succeeded Nasser in 1970. He launched the 1973 October War against Israel, but made peace in 1979. He was assassinated by Islamic extremists in Cairo in 1981.

Savir, Uri Savir was born in Jerusalem in 1953. He became a lawyer and negotiated the 1993 Oslo agreement for Israel. Savir is a career diplomat who is now head of the Peres Center for Peace.

Shamir, Yitzhak Shamir was born in Poland in 1915, and moved to Palestine in 1935. He joined the resistance against the British authorities. He was elected to the Knesset in 1973, and became Likud prime minister in 1983. Shamir was defeated in the 1992 election and left politics in 1996.

Sharon, Ariel Sharon is an Israeli politician and former soldier. He was born in Mandate Palestine in 1928. He was elected to the Knesset in 1973, and became minister of defence in 1981. Sharon was the head of the Likud Party in 1999, and became prime minister in 2001.

Truman, Harry S 33rd president of the USA (1945–1953). Truman was born in 1884, and died in 1953. He backed the UN resolution in 1947 calling for Palestine to be partitioned. This led to the establishment of the State of Israel in 1948.

Wilson, Woodrow 28th president of the USA (1913–1921). Wilson was born in 1856, and died in 1924. He helped found the League of Nations and set up the mandate system under which Great Britain ruled Palestine.

Find Out More

BOOKS FOR YOUNGER READERS

The Arab-Israeli Conflict, (Troubled World Series), Ivan Minnis (Raintree, 2003)
Historical facts about the conflict between Israel and the Arabs presented in an approachable way.

The Israeli-Palestinian Conflict, John Boaz (Greenhaven Press, 2004)
A book giving a wide range of viewpoints on this controversial issue.

Three Wishes: Palestinian and Israeli Children Speak, Deborah Ellis (Groundwood Books, 2004)
A collection of personal stories from young Palestinians and Israelis between the ages of 8 and 18 that shows how war affects their lives.

BOOKS FOR OLDER READERS

The Case for Israel, Alan Dershowitz (John Wiley & Sons, 2003)
A defence of Israel's case and its arguments against Palestinian claims.

A Concise History of the Arab-Israeli Conflict, Ian J. Bickerton and Carla L. Klausner (Prentice Hall, 2001)
A basic, factual history of the conflict. Good for reference.

A History of Modern Palestine: One Land, Two Peoples, Ilan Pappé (Cambridge University Press, 2003)
A balanced look at the history of Israel and Palestine by an Israeli historian.

Palestine, Joe Sacco (Jonathan Cape, 2004)
A 'graphic book' about the Israel-Palestine conflict, from a viewpoint that is sympathetic to the Palestinians.

War Without End: Israelis, Palestinians and the Struggle for a Promised Land, Anton La Guardia (Griffin, 2003)
A journalist's view of the people and issues behind the conflict. The author spent many years in Jerusalem.

ADDRESSES TO WRITE TO

If you want to find out more about Israel and Palestine, try contacting these organizations:

IN THE UK

The London Middle East Institute
Room 479
School of Oriental and African Studies
University of London
Russell Square
London WC1H OXG

The Royal Institute of International Affairs
Chatham House
10 St James's Square
London SW1Y 4LE

International Institute for Strategic Studies
Arundel House
13–15 Arundel Street
Temple Place
London WC2R 3DX

Council for Arab-British Understanding
1 Gough Square
London EC4A 3DE

IN AUSTRALIA

The Centre for Middle East and North African Studies
Macquarie University
Sydney 2109

The Centre for Middle Eastern and Central Asian Studies
Australian National University
Canberra ACT 0200

Index

Index

Titles in *The Middle East* series include:

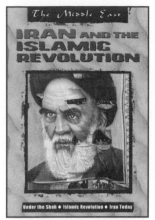

Hardback   1-844-43206-8

Hardback   1-844-43205-X

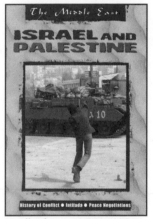

Hardback   1-844-43204-1

Hardback   1-844-43203-3

Hardback   1-844-43207-6

Find out about other titles from Raintree on our website www.raintreepublishers.co.uk